Lorikeet's Garden Playground
Second Edition

Rainbow Lorikeets are so full of life, their fun-loving, mischievous nature is captivating.

This story, the fifth in the Lorikeet's Book Series for young readers, is based on a family of Rainbow Lorikeets who visit a secluded garden regularly. Another Lorikeet family, different in colour are not welcomed.

Through my words and the creative vision of Lillian Falzon, whose illustrations brought these characters to life, I hope you enjoy a peek into the adventures of this quirky, colourful family.

Lawrence the Rainbow Lorikeet and his partner Loretta are perched on the edge of the tree cavity where they made their home.

Lawrence is a very handsome Lorikeet and he knows it, he is preening his lustrous green coat and red and yellow vest.

Loretta helps by combing his pastel green collar and blue cap with her red beak.

Since the day he discovered the garden with the trays of sunflower seeds, Lawrence takes his family there as often as possible for a treat.

Lawrence stands tall and puffs out his chest, feeling proud as a father who finds food and protects his family from danger and unwanted intruders.

The sun is now softly lighting the morning sky.
Lawrence, preened to perfection, asks Loretta to wake
the chicks for breakfast.

Loretta chirps and whistles and the chicks slowly wake
up stretching out their green wings displaying the
red and yellow lining of their cloaks. They shake their
bodies until they look like brightly coloured fluffy balls.

Larry the youngest is a little slower waking than the others so Loretta gives him a gentle nudge with her wing.

Lawrence lets out a huge screech, Loretta and the family take flight and follow him to the garden.

They all settle on to trays and other families of Rainbow Lorikeets join them as they have before.

Lawrence, "Mister Bossy Boots" won't allow other families to be on the feeder he shares with Loretta and ruffles his feathers and leaps forward with his beak on his chest, looking scary, making sure the other lorikeets know they are not wanted on his tray.

The Lorikeets are noisy eaters, chirping, screeching and chattering all the time.

Other males like Lawrence, bully other birds until a fight breaks out resulting in a lot of screeching, wing flapping and commotion.

For fun, the Lorikeets fly off through the trees and circle back to the garden.

On this occasion four Scaly-breasted Lorikeets return to the garden with them unnoticed. The Scaly-breasted Lorikeets are similar in size and shape to the Rainbow Lorikeets but they have brilliant green jackets and yellow and green vests.

Stewart, the leader of the Scaly-breasted Lorikeets and his mates, Sam, Simon and Sylvester, are checking the area for safety before the females arrive.

Stewart and Sylvester fly to a tray and as it happens, it is the tray where Lawrence and Loretta are.

As usual, "Mister Bossy Boots", Lawrence gives them their marching orders.

He puffs out his red and yellow chest and lurches at Stewart and Sylvester shooing them off the tray where he and Loretta are quietly enjoying the feast of sunflower seeds.

The female Scaly-breasted Lorikeets Sarah, Susan, Simone and Samantha quietly fly in to the garden to join Stewart and the others, so now there are eight.

As they have arrived without an invitation, the Rainbow Lorikeets won't allow them to share a tray. The flock of Scaly-breasted Lorikeets happily fly to the area underneath the trays and feast on the seeds that have fallen to the ground.

The Scaly-breasted Lorikeets have their fill of seeds then fly away together leaving as quietly as they came, the red, orange and green lining of their jackets glow in the morning sun.

The Rainbow Lorikeets are again the only birds in the garden.

They continue to chatter, chirp and fly in and out of the trees enjoying the garden as their own personal playground.

Lorikeet's Garden Playground

ISBN

979-1-7640295-9-9 (Paperback)

978-1-7642196-0-0 (eBook)

www.ingramcontent.com/pod-product-compliance
Lightning Source LLC
Chambersburg PA
CBHW060842270326

41933CB00002B/167